U.S.A. TRAVEL GUIDES

INDIANA

BY ANN HEINRICHS • ILLUSTRATED BY MATT KANIA

The Child's World®
childsworld.com

Published by The Child's World®
1980 Lookout Drive • Mankato, MN 56003-1705
800-599-READ • www.childsworld.com

ISBN 9781503819542
LCCN 2016961130

Printing

Printed in the United States of America
PA02334

Ann Heinrichs is the author of more than 100 books for children and young adults. She has also enjoyed successful careers as a children's book editor and an advertising copywriter. Ann grew up in Fort Smith, Arkansas, and lives in Chicago, Illinois.

post card

About the Author
Ann Heinrichs

Matt Kania loves maps and, as a kid, dreamed of making them. In school he studied geography and cartography, and today he makes maps for a living. Matt's favorite thing about drawing maps is learning about the places they represent. Many of the maps he has created can be found in books, magazines, videos, Web sites, and public places.

post card

About the
Map Illustrator
Matt Kania

On the cover: Take a tour of the capitol building when you visit Indianapolis.

OUR INDIANA TRIP

INDIANA

Are you up for a trip through Indiana? You'll find it's a great place to explore!

You'll ride a **canal** boat and watch car races. You'll hang out with **pioneers**. You'll watch people making glass. You'll make big bubbles and play with your shadow. You'll climb sand dunes much taller than a house. You'll see wild turkeys and deer. And you'll make candles and milk a cow!

Is this your kind of fun? Then settle in and buckle up. We're on our way!

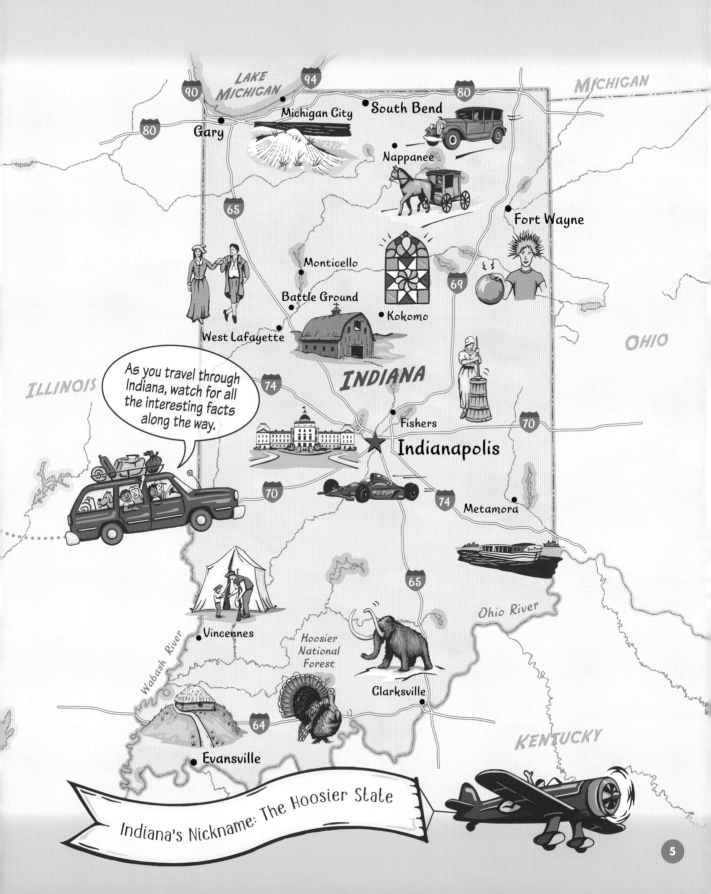

As you travel through Indiana, watch for all the interesting facts along the way.

Indiana's Nickname: The Hoosier State

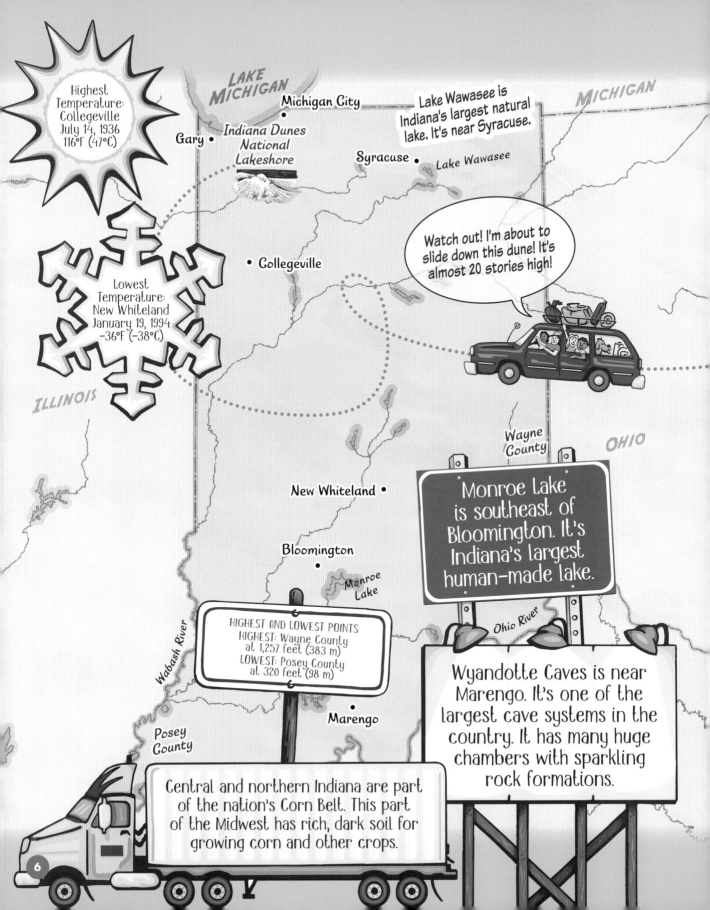

LAKE MICHIGAN

MICHIGAN

Highest Temperature: Collegeville July 14, 1936 116°F (47°C)

Michigan City

Gary

Indiana Dunes National Lakeshore

Lake Wawasee is Indiana's largest natural lake. It's near Syracuse.

Syracuse

Lake Wawasee

Lowest Temperature: New Whiteland January 19, 1994 –36°F (–38°C)

Collegeville

Watch out! I'm about to slide down this dune! It's almost 20 stories high!

ILLINOIS

Wayne County

OHIO

New Whiteland

Monroe Lake is southeast of Bloomington. It's Indiana's largest human-made lake.

Bloomington

Monroe Lake

HIGHEST AND LOWEST POINTS
HIGHEST: Wayne County at 1,257 feet (383 m)
LOWEST: Posey County at 320 feet (98 m)

Ohio River

Wabash River

Marengo

Wyandotte Caves is near Marengo. It's one of the largest cave systems in the country. It has many huge chambers with sparkling rock formations.

Posey County

Central and northern Indiana are part of the nation's Corn Belt. This part of the Midwest has rich, dark soil for growing corn and other crops.

EXPLORING THE INDIANA DUNES

Hike along miles of beaches. Explore the marshy wetlands. Roam through a forest. Or climb a sand dune.

You're exploring Indiana Dunes National Lakeshore! It runs along the Lake Michigan shore. It stretches from Gary to Michigan City.

Northwest Indiana faces Lake Michigan. This lake is one of the five Great Lakes. Fertile plains cover central Indiana. Its rich soil makes great farmland.

Southern Indiana is hilly. In some places, streams flow underground. The streams have created many spooky caves. The Ohio River runs along Indiana's southern border. The Wabash River flows into it. The Wabash forms part of Indiana's western border.

You'll find miles of trails to explore at Indiana Dunes National Lakeshore.

Sneak softly through Hoosier National Forest. A shy deer may peek out at you. Foxes, woodchucks, and squirrels scurry here and there. You might come upon a female wild turkey. Her babies waddle along behind her.

Near a stream, you may see beavers. They build their lodges with sticks and grass. Herons and egrets live near the water, too. Hawks and eagles soar high overhead.

Hoosier National Forest covers much of southern Indiana. It's a great place for watching wildlife. The forest is made of four big sections. Its northern end is near Nashville. Its southern end is near Tell City.

Many deer and other wild animals live in Indiana's forests.

Female turkeys are called hens. Their babies are called poults.

Turkey quiz time! What are male turkeys called? They're called gobblers or toms!

LAKE MICHIGAN

MICHIGAN

OHIO

ILLINOIS

STATE FLOWER
PEONY

STATE TREE
TULIP TREE
(YELLOW POPLAR)

STATE BIRD
CARDINAL

• Battle Ground

Muscatatuck National Wildlife Refuge is near Seymour. River otters were introduced there in 1995. The refuge is also known for its many waterbirds.

• Nashville

• Seymour

Madison •

The National Park Service has three sites in Indiana.

Hoosier National Forest

Big Oaks National Wildlife Refuge is near Madison. Many kinds of birds, bats, butterflies, and mammals live there.

• Tell City

KENTUCKY

Wolf Park in Battle Ground is home to a pack of wolves. You'll hear the wolves howl at night. Foxes, bison, and coyotes live there, too.

Who Lived Here before Europeans Arrived? Delaware, Huron, Kickapoo, Miami, Mound Builders, Munsee, Piankashaw, Potawatomi, Shawnee, and Wea

Thousands of Mound Builders lived at Angel Mounds.

The Mound Builders played a game called chunkey. Players rolled a stone. They threw a spear at the point where they thought the stone would stop.

The Pokagon Band of Potawatomi tribe holds the Kee-Boon-Mein-Kaa Powwow in South Bend. It's a huckleberry harvest festival.

People first lived at Angel Mounds in about 1100. They began leaving in about 1400. Historians aren't sure why they left.

LAKE MICHIGAN

MICHIGAN

• South Bend

ILLINOIS

OHIO

KENTUCKY

• Evansville

ANGEL MOUNDS IN EVANSVILLE

Stroll through the village houses. Life-size figures are all around you. Some are hunting or making meals. Others are playing games. You're visiting Angel Mounds in Evansville.

Native Americans called Mound Builders lived here approximately 1,000 years ago. You'll see the huge earthen mounds they created. Chiefs and nobles built homes on the mounds. Some mounds had temples on top. Priests held religious ceremonies there.

People from miles around traveled to Angel Mounds. They came to trade goods and attend ceremonies. More than 20,000 Native Americans live in Indiana today. The main Native American tribes in Indiana today are the Miami Nation, the Wea, the Pokagon Band of Potawatomi, and the Upper Kispoko Band of the Shawnee Nation.

Many mounds served as temples. Mound builders brought offerings to these mounds.

THE FEAST OF THE HUNTERS' MOON

Make a hand-dipped candle. Listen to traditional Native American stories from members of the Wea and other Northeast tribes. Or try some rabbit stew. It's the Feast of the Hunters' Moon! This festival recalls Indiana's olden days. It takes place at Fort Ouiatenon in West Lafayette.

Fur traders were early European explorers in Indiana. They were Frenchmen from Canada, to the north. They traded goods with the Wea and other Eastern Woodlands tribes for furs. Fort Ouiatenon was built in 1717. It was a fur-trading post.

Every fall, the French and Native Americans gathered there. They celebrated the Feast of the Hunters' Moon. It was a chance to build friendships. People shared their stories, food, and games.

Listen to French colonial music at the Feast of the Hunters' Moon.

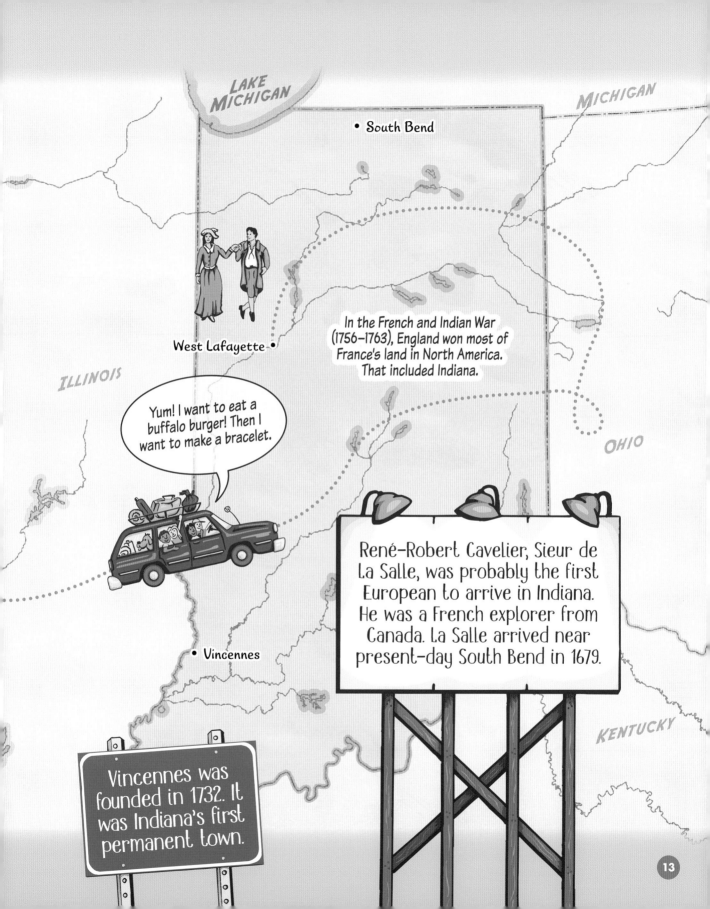

LAKE MICHIGAN

MICHIGAN

• South Bend

West Lafayette •

ILLINOIS

In the French and Indian War
(1756–1763), England won most of
France's land in North America.
That included Indiana.

Yum! I want to eat a
buffalo burger! Then I
want to make a bracelet.

OHIO

• Vincennes

René-Robert Cavelier, Sieur de
La Salle, was probably the first
European to arrive in Indiana.
He was a French explorer from
Canada. La Salle arrived near
present-day South Bend in 1679.

Vincennes was
founded in 1732. It
was Indiana's first
permanent town.

KENTUCKY

Indiana was the 19th state to enter the Union. It joined on December 11, 1816.

Hey, look! We can try trundling the hoop, stilt walking, and ninepins! Kids played these games in the 1700s.

The first public **subscription** library in Indiana opened in Vincennes in 1807.

The British surrendered Fort Sackville on February 25, 1779.

• Vincennes

The United States set up the Northwest Territory in 1787. It included what is now Indiana as well as four other states.

The Spirit of Vincennes Rendezvous takes place at George Rogers Clark National Historical Park in Vincennes.

THE SPIRIT OF VINCENNES RENDEZVOUS

Pow! Cannons are booming. **Muskets** are firing. It's the Spirit of Vincennes **Rendezvous**!

This event celebrates a great victory in 1779. The Revolutionary War (1775–1783) was going on. **Colonists** were fighting for freedom from British rule.

British troops had captured Fort Sackville at Vincennes. George Rogers Clark hoped to win it back. His soldiers snuck into Vincennes and surprised the British. At last, they won the fort!

Colonial times come to life at the rendezvous. People dress like the settlers did. They act out battles and demonstrate colonial crafts. Kids ride ponies and play colonial games. Drop by and enjoy the fun!

That's a lot of smoke! Watch a battle reenactment at the Spirit of Vincennes Rendezvous.

THE STATE CAPITOL IN INDIANAPOLIS

The state capitol is a grand building. And no wonder. It's the center of state government! Many important decisions are made here. These decisions affect everyone in the state.

Indiana has three branches of government. All three branches meet in the capitol. One branch passes state laws. Its members belong to the General Assembly. Another branch makes sure the laws are carried out. The governor heads this branch. Judges make up the third branch. They decide whether laws have been broken.

Indiana's state motto is "The Crossroads of America."

The Indiana state capitol was built in the late 1800s.

LAKE MICHIGAN

MICHIGAN

OHIO

Is the General Assembly meeting now? If it is, a tour guide can take us in to watch the lawmakers in action.

ILLINOIS

★ Indianapolis

Vincennes was the first capital of the Indiana Territory. Corydon became the capital in 1813. Statehood came in 1816. Then in 1825, Indianapolis became the capital.

• Vincennes

William Henry Harrison was the first governor of the Indiana Territory. His house in Vincennes was called Grouseland. Harrison became the ninth president in 1841. He died after only one month in office.

• Corydon

Benjamin Harrison was the 23rd U.S. president (1889-1893). He was William Henry Harrison's grandson. Born in Ohio, Benjamin lived in Indiana as an adult.

KENTUCKY

Welcome to Indianapolis, the capital of Indiana!

LAKE MICHIGAN

MICHIGAN

ILLINOIS

• Battle Ground

Let's chat with the fur trader at the trading post! Let's weave a basket and walk on stilts!

• Fishers

★ Indianapolis

OHIO

The Indiana State Museum in Indianapolis houses photographs and other items related to Abraham Lincoln.

Abraham Lincoln (1809-1865) was the 16th U.S. president. He lived in Indiana from age seven to 21. The Lincoln family farm is now Lincoln Boyhood National Memorial in Lincoln City.

Conner Prairie holds classes that teach kids many pioneer crafts.

• Lincoln City

KENTUCKY

Tippecanoe Battlefield is in Battle Ground. General William Henry Harrison's army defeated the Shawnee Native Americans there in 1811.

CONNER PRAIRIE INTERACTIVE HISTORY PARK

What was life like in Indiana in the 1800s? Step back in time and see for yourself. Just visit Conner Prairie in Fishers!

You'll grind corn in the Lenape Indian Camp. You'll see how European settlers lived when you visit Prairietown. You'll milk a cow and churn butter. You'll see that people in the 1800s really kept busy!

Many pioneers moved into Indiana. They had heard how rich the soil was. They cleared land and planted crops. But the Lenape and other Native Americans had lived on the land long before the European settlers came. Native Americans and settlers often clashed.

The Native Americans didn't want to lose their homeland, but they did. Some of it was taken after they lost battles. Other land was purchased by the U.S. government. The Native Americans were forced out.

Discover what life in Indiana was once like for both Native Americans and pioneers at Conner Prairie.

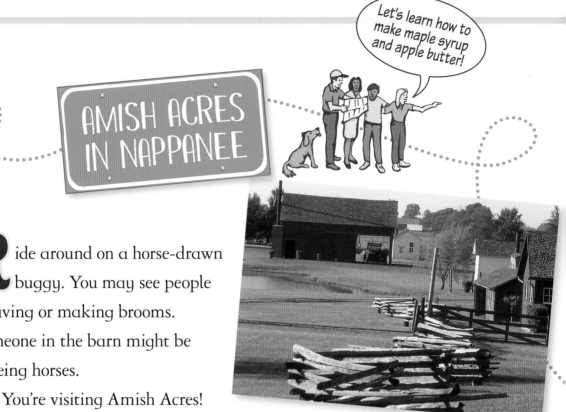

Let's learn how to make maple syrup and apple butter!

AMISH ACRES IN NAPPANEE

Ride around on a horse-drawn buggy. You may see people weaving or making brooms. Someone in the barn might be shoeing horses.

You're visiting Amish Acres! There you learn how Indiana's Amish people live.

The Amish are a religious group. They believe that living simply brings them closer to their faith. They live on farms and ride horse-drawn buggies instead of cars. They don't use electricity or other modern devices.

The Amish first came to Indiana in 1839. They were often misunderstood and not welcomed in Europe. They hoped for a better life in the United States.

More than 40,000 Amish people live in Indiana today. The Amish are among the fastest-growing population groups in the United States. Today they live in 30 U.S. states as well as in Canada.

Three generations of Amish families have lived on the farm in Amish Acres.

The Pierogi Fest is in Whiting. It celebrates the pierogi. That's an eastern European dumpling with meat or vegetables inside.

Indiana's German festivals include Schweizer Fest in Tell City, Strassenfest in Jasper, and Oktoberfest in Seymour.

In 2016, 6,633,053 people lived in Indiana. It's the 17th-largest state by population.

Amish Heritage Furniture is in Middlebury. You can watch the Amish craftsmen at work. They build a single piece of furniture at a time.

Jacob Ammann founded the Amish church in 1693. Its early members lived in Switzerland and Germany. The Amish in the United States are their **descendants.**

Population of Largest Cities

Indianapolis	853,173
Fort Wayne	260,326
Evansville	119,943

Whiting • — Middlebury

• Nappanee

• Fort Wayne

★ Indianapolis

Seymour •

Jasper •

• Evansville — Tell City

ILLINOIS

LAKE MICHIGAN

MICHIGAN

OHIO

KENTUCKY

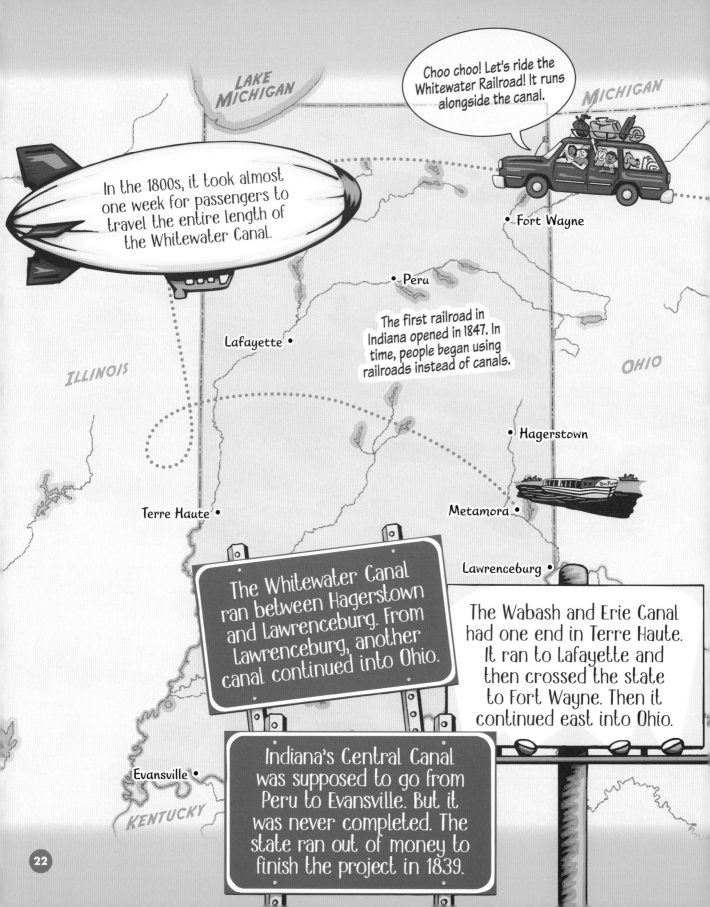

Hop aboard the *Ben Franklin III*. You board this canal boat in Metamora. There's a horse walking along the shore. He's pulling your boat!

Then check out the mill. You'll see it grind corn into cornmeal. The canal waters turn its mill wheel around. You're exploring the Whitewater Canal!

People began digging this canal in the 1830s. Canals were great for transportation. Farmers used them to ship goods. That was much faster than land travel. People traveled on canal boats, too. That was easier than riding through the wilderness!

The Duck Creek Aqueduct over the Whitewater Canal is a covered wooden bridge. It was built in 1846.

See an old covered wagon. Walk on, and look at some antique cars. You'll even see some presidents' coaches. You're touring the Studebaker National Museum!

Clement and Henry Studebaker were brothers. They opened a horse-drawn wagon shop in 1852. But they saw what the future held—cars! They built an electric car in 1902. Next, they developed cars that ran on gasoline. The Studebaker company built cars until 1966.

Many other **industries** helped Indiana grow. An oil-**refining** plant opened in Whiting in 1889. It produced gasoline for cars. Steel mills opened in Gary, too.

They don't make cars like this anymore! Check out some cool cars at the Studebaker National Museum.

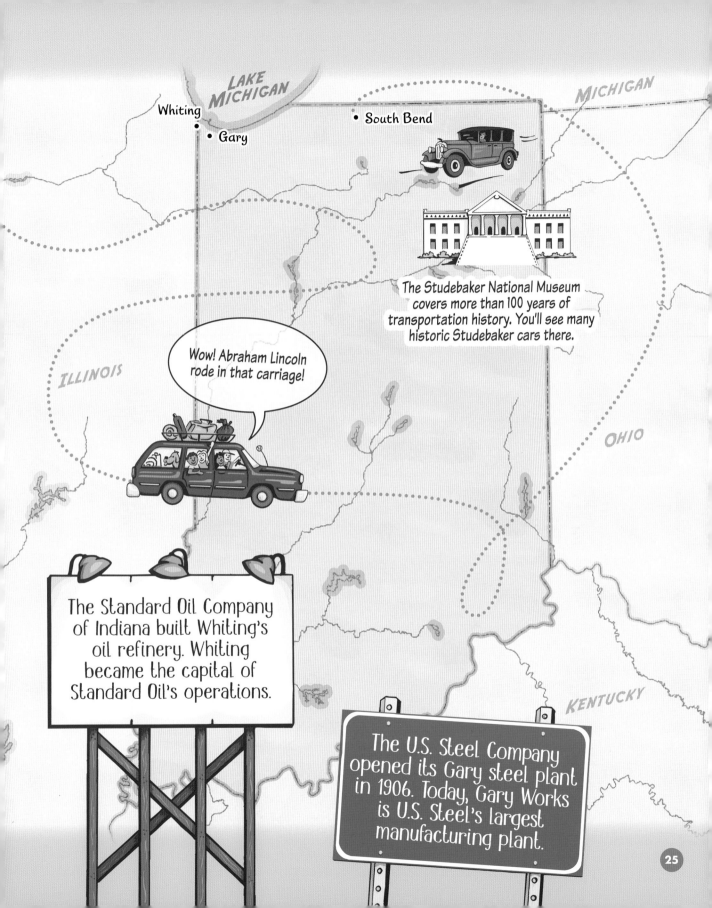

LAKE MICHIGAN

Whiting

Gary

South Bend

MICHIGAN

ILLINOIS

OHIO

KENTUCKY

The Studebaker National Museum covers more than 100 years of transportation history. You'll see many historic Studebaker cars there.

Wow! Abraham Lincoln rode in that carriage!

The Standard Oil Company of Indiana built Whiting's oil refinery. Whiting became the capital of Standard Oil's operations.

The U.S. Steel Company opened its Gary steel plant in 1906. Today, Gary Works is U.S. Steel's largest manufacturing plant.

LAKE MICHIGAN

MICHIGAN

The first Indianapolis 500 car race took place in 1911.

Guess what the winner does after the race? Drinks milk in Victory Lane! The winner did that in 1936. Now all winners do it!

Marion •

ILLINOIS

The Indiana Basketball Hall of Fame is in New Castle.

• New Castle

OHIO

★ Indianapolis

STP

Indianapolis 500 racers go around the track 200 times. Their total distance is 500 miles (805 km).

Cartoonist Jim Davis created the comic strip *Garfield*. Davis was born on a cow farm near Marion.

The NCAA Hall of Champions is in Indianapolis. It celebrates the history of college sports.

KENTUCKY

THE INDIANAPOLIS 500

Vroom! And they're off! The colorful cars zoom around the track. Some go more than 200 miles (320 km) an hour. It's the Indianapolis 500!

This is a world-famous car race. Racing fans come from all over to watch. It takes place in Speedway, near Indianapolis.

Indiana is also known for its basketball games. High school games are especially popular. State tournament time in March is wild. It's called Hoosier Hysteria!

For quieter fun, people enjoy the outdoors. They hike along the dunes or through forests.

Watch cars fly by at the Indianapolis 500!

THE FARM AT PROPHETSTOWN

What goes on inside the barn? Horses munch on their hay. A farmer milks a cow. And cats stand by, hoping for some milk!

Now look around the farmyard. Workers load hay onto wagons with pitchforks. You might see new baby horses or sheep. You can pet them if they don't run away!

You're exploring the Farm at Prophetstown. It's just like a farm in the 1920s. Farming has always been important in Indiana. Corn and soybeans are the top crops today. Some of that corn ends up as popcorn!

You'll see horses and all kinds of farm animals at the Farm at Prophetstown.

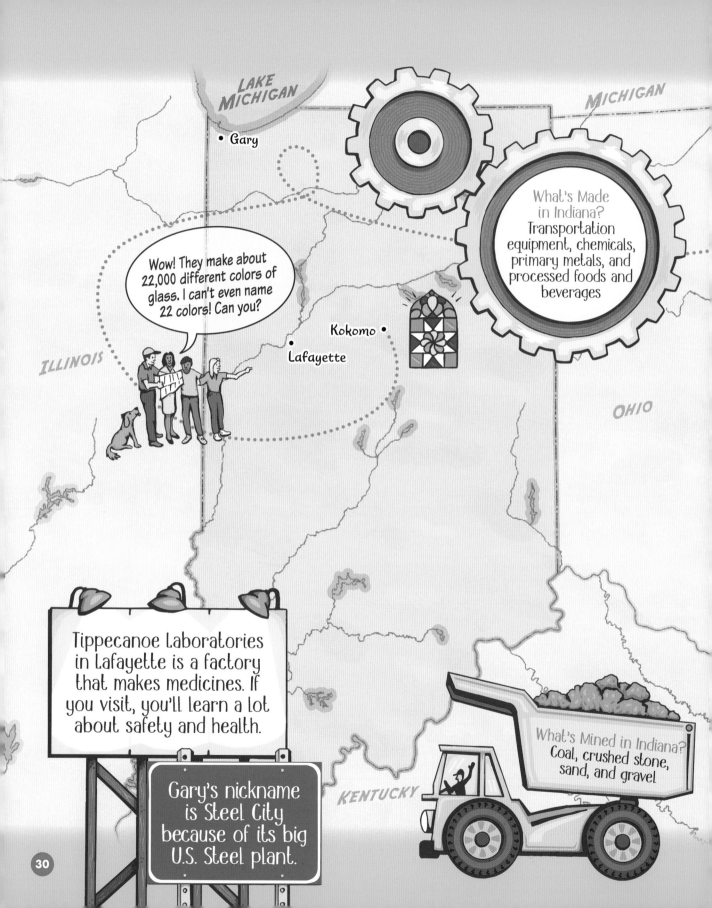

Wow! They make about 22,000 different colors of glass. I can't even name 22 colors! Can you?

What's Made in Indiana? Transportation equipment, chemicals, primary metals, and processed foods and beverages

Tippecanoe Laboratories in Lafayette is a factory that makes medicines. If you visit, you'll learn a lot about safety and health.

Gary's nickname is Steel City because of its big U.S. Steel plant.

What's Mined in Indiana? Coal, crushed stone, sand, and gravel

Have you ever seen stained-glass windows? Want to learn how they're made? Just tour Kokomo Opalescent Glass.

You'll see fiery furnaces melting the glass. Workers pick up melted glass with big **ladles**. They pour different colors of glass together. Rollers roll the glass into sheets. It's hard work. But the results are beautiful!

Glass is only one of Indiana's factory goods. Transportation equipment is the leading factory product. That includes cars, recreational vehicles, and airplane parts. Steel is a major product, too. Most steel plants are in cities along Lake Michigan. Their smokestacks rise high into the sky.

No other state makes more steel than Indiana.

These men are making glass at an Indiana factory in 1908.

Find out how it would feel to walk on the moon. See how electricity can make your hair stand straight out. And try riding a bicycle that's 25 feet (8 meters) off the ground!

Do all this and more at Science Central in Fort Wayne. It's an amazing science museum. Kids love to explore and learn new things there. They discover the wonders of science!

Scientific discoveries brought Indiana into the modern world. Hundreds of Indiana companies make computer-related equipment. Some equipment makes factories run. Other equipment creates faster ways to communicate. And some equipment has medical uses. Inventors of all these devices began as curious kids!

Have fun with funhouse mirrors at Fort Wayne's Science Central.

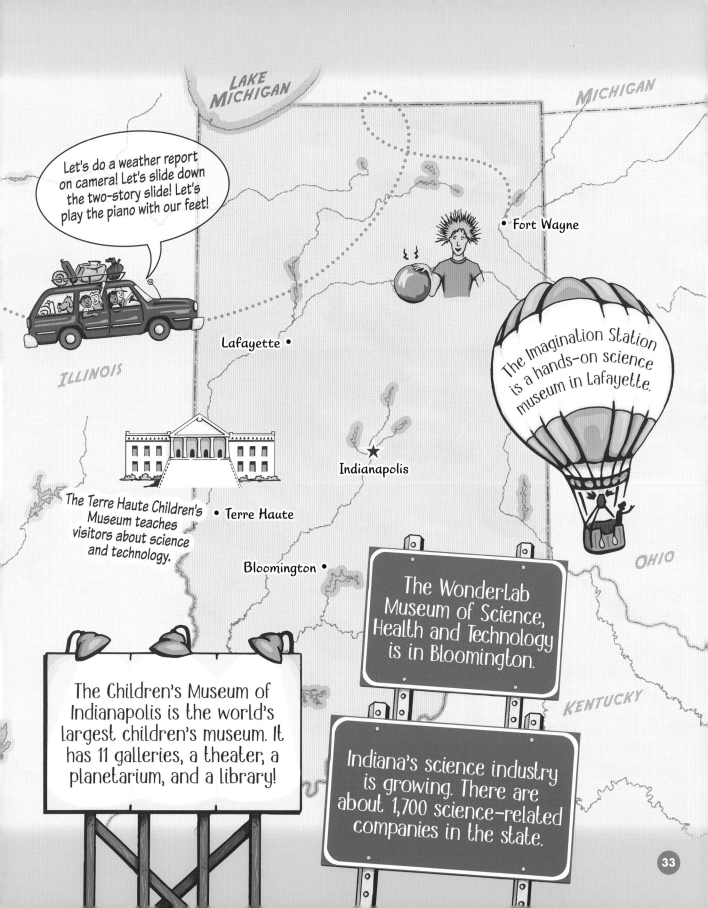

Let's do a weather report on camera! Let's slide down the two-story slide! Let's play the piano with our feet!

LAKE MICHIGAN

MICHIGAN

• Fort Wayne

Lafayette •

The Imagination Station is a hands-on science museum in Lafayette.

ILLINOIS

★ Indianapolis

The Terre Haute Children's Museum teaches visitors about science and technology.

• Terre Haute

Bloomington •

OHIO

The WonderLab Museum of Science, Health and Technology is in Bloomington.

KENTUCKY

The Children's Museum of Indianapolis is the world's largest children's museum. It has 11 galleries, a theater, a planetarium, and a library!

Indiana's science industry is growing. There are about 1,700 science-related companies in the state.

FOSSILS AT THE FALLS OF THE OHIO

Explore caves lined with **fossils**. See a wooly **mammoth** skeleton. You are visiting the Falls of the Ohio State Park.

Thousands of fossils were discovered in this area. Some are 390 million years old!

This site is in Clarksville. It's right by the Ohio River. An ancient sea once covered this area. Land and sea creatures left their remains behind.

You'll see all kinds of fossils here. One fish was 23 feet (7 m) long! Good thing you weren't going swimming millions of years ago!

Learn about Indiana's prehistoric past at the Falls of the Ohio State Park Interpretive Center.

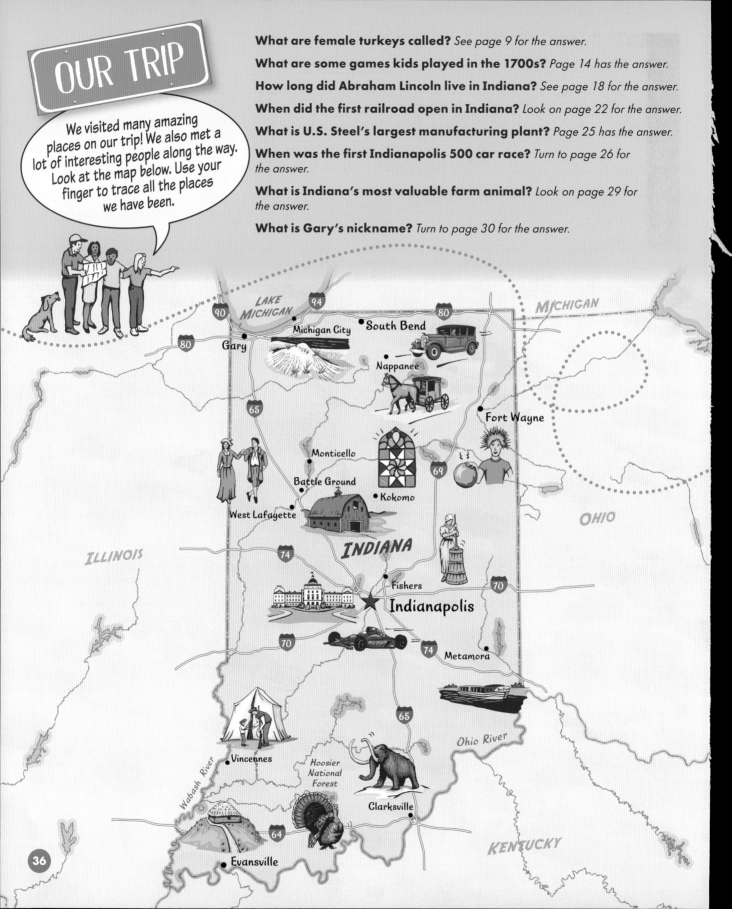

OUR TRIP

We visited many amazing places on our trip! We also met a lot of interesting people along the way. Look at the map below. Use your finger to trace all the places we have been.

What are female turkeys called? *See page 9 for the answer.*

What are some games kids played in the 1700s? *Page 14 has the answer.*

How long did Abraham Lincoln live in Indiana? *See page 18 for the answer.*

When did the first railroad open in Indiana? *Look on page 22 for the answer.*

What is U.S. Steel's largest manufacturing plant? *Page 25 has the answer.*

When was the first Indianapolis 500 car race? *Turn to page 26 for the answer.*

What is Indiana's most valuable farm animal? *Look on page 29 for the answer.*

What is Gary's nickname? *Turn to page 30 for the answer.*

LAKE MICHIGAN

MICHIGAN

90   94   80

Gary   Michigan City   South Bend

Nappanee

Fort Wayne

65

Monticello

Battle Ground   Kokomo

69

West Lafayette

INDIANA

OHIO

74

Fishers   70

Indianapolis

ILLINOIS

70   74   Metamora

65

Ohio River

Vincennes

Hoosier National Forest

Wabash River

Clarksville

64

KENTUCKY

Evansville

State flag

State seal

STATE SYMBOLS

State bird: Cardinal

State flower: Peony

State poem: "Indiana" by Arthur Franklin Mapes

State river: Wabash River

State stone: Salem limestone

State tree: Tulip tree (yellow poplar)

STATE SONG

"ON THE BANKS OF THE WABASH, FAR AWAY"
Words and music by Paul Dresser

'Round my Indiana homestead wave the cornfields,
In the distance loom the woodlands clear and cool.
Oftentimes my thoughts revert to scenes of childhood,
Where I first received my lessons, nature's school.
But one thing there is missing in the picture,
Without her face it seems so incomplete.
I long to see my mother in the doorway,
As she stood there years ago, her boy to greet.

Chorus:
Oh, the moonlight's fair tonight along the Wabash,
From the fields there comes the breath of new-mown
    hay.
Through the sycamores the candle lights are gleaming,
On the banks of the Wabash, far away.

Many years have passed since I strolled by the river,
Arm in arm, with sweetheart Mary by my side,
It was there I tried to tell her that I loved her,
It was there I begged of her to be my bride.

Long years have passed since I strolled thro' the
    churchyard.
She's sleeping there, my angel, Mary dear,
I loved her, but she thought I didn't mean it,
Still I'd give my future were she only here.

That was a great trip! We have traveled all over Indiana. There are a few places that we didn't have time for, though. Next time, we plan to visit Indiana Beach Amusement Park in Monticello. It has roller coasters, rides, a lake, and a sand beach. There is even a giant water park!

FAMOUS PEOPLE

Bird, Larry (1956–), basketball player and coach

Bridwell, Norman (1928–2014), children's author and illustrator

Cabot, Meg (1967–), author

Coffin, Levi (1798–1877), abolitionist

Davis, Jim (1945–), cartoonist

Dillinger, John (1903–1934), gangster

Fraser, Brendan (1968–), actor

Gordon, Jeff (1971–), NASCAR racer

Grissom, Virgil (1926–1967), astronaut

Harrison, Benjamin (1833–1901), 23rd U.S. president

Jackson, Michael (1958–2009), singer

Lambert, Adam (1982–), singer

Letterman, David (1947–), comedian and television host

Mellencamp, John (1951–), singer and songwriter

Naylor, Phyllis Reynolds (1933–), children's author

Pyle, Ernie (1900–1945), journalist

Riley, James Whitcomb (1849–1916), poet

Stewart, Tony (1971–), NASCAR racer

Vonnegut, Kurt, Jr. (1922–2007), author

Walker, Madam C. J. (1867–1919), businesswoman and millionaire

Warren Jr., Chris (1990–), actor

White, Ryan (1971–1990), young AIDS victim and activist

Wright, Wilbur (1867–1912), inventor and pilot

WORDS TO KNOW

canal (kuh-NAL) a long waterway dug by humans

colonists (KOL-uh-nihsts) people who settle in a land with ties to a mother country

descendants (di-SEND-uhnts) a person's children, grandchildren, great-grandchildren, and so on

fossils (FOSS-uhlz) prints or remains of plants and animals that lived long ago

industries (IN-duh-streez) types of businesses

ladles (LAY-duhlz) big spoons that are like bowls with long handles

mammoth (MAMM-uth) a huge animal similar to an elephant that lived a long time ago

muskets (MUSS-kits) early types of rifles

pioneers (pie-uh-NEERZ) the first people to move into an unsettled area

refining (rih-FINE-ing) a process that removes extra material and cleans the remains

rendezvous (RON-day-voo) French word for a meeting

subscription (suhb-SKRIP-shuhn) a service that people regularly pay money for

TO LEARN MORE

IN THE LIBRARY

Brezina, Corona. *Indiana: Past and Present*. New York, NY: Rosen Central, 2010.

Helweg, Laura. *Eastern Great Lakes: Indiana, Michigan, Ohio*. Broomall, PA: Mason Crest, 2015.

Jones, Kadeem. *Shawnee*. New York, NY: PowerKids Press, 2016.

Ryan, Patrick. *Indiana: The Hoosier State*. Minneapolis, MN: Bellwether Media, 2014.

ON THE WEB

Visit our Web site for links about Indiana:

childsworld.com/links

Note to Parents, Teachers, and Librarians: We routinely verify our Web links to make sure they are safe and active sites. So encourage your readers to check them out!

PLACES TO VISIT OR CONTACT

Indiana Office of Tourism Development

visitindianatourism.com
One North Capitol, Suite 600
Indianapolis, IN 46204
317/232-8860
For more information about traveling in Indiana

Indiana Historical Society

indianahistory.org
450 West Ohio Street
Indianapolis, IN 46202
317/232-1882
For more information about the history of Indiana

Indiana covers 36,420 square miles (94,327 sq km). It's the 38th-largest state in size.

INDEX

Bye, Hoosier State.
We had a great time.
We'll come back soon!